I0428715

DO TO ANIMALS...

BY HANNAH FAYE

Copyright © 2012 by Hannah Faye
Copyright © 2016 Revision

All rights reserved under Copyright laws. This book was published in the United States of America and no copies or distribution shall be made without the written consent of the author. Visit www. hannahfayewrites.weebly.com for more information and to connect with Hannah Faye.

"Do to _____ as you would have them do to you. You fill in the blank." -Hannah Faye

"Nobody really knows what animals are thinking...nobody"- Veterinarian of 27 years

Chapters

Introduction

My name is Dr. Phyllis McClune, DVM. I was a veterinarian for nearly twenty-two years before the accident happened that would change my life forever. In that time I've acquired a wide range of experience working with all types of animals. For the first five years I tended to livestock, followed by seven years of treating exotic animals at zoos. I spent the remaining ten years as an equine vet, mainly treating horses. As a full-time vet, I enjoyed spending most of my day visiting clients before returning home to my own animals, which included three dogs, two cats, two horses, a parrot and several fish. I'm 52 years of age, single and still without any children, but with so many animals, who needs children? I take very good care of them. I love them just as a mother would love her own children. We're one big, happy family. This is the way I've always wanted it...being surrounded by animals, you see. Every since I was a child I've always loved them so much. I remember having more animal friends than human ones. At one point, my mother was concerned about my "obsession" with them, as she called it, enough to admit me for psychological evaluation. Imagine that. Of course, they found nothing wrong with me. I told her so. I told her there was nothing wrong with me. I just found the time I spent with animals to be much more worthwhile than the time I spent with humans. No offense. I suppose it was my love for animals that led me to acquire so many of my own. Animals *are* my life. I even wrote about them in my spare time and managed to publish a few short, literary pieces, but nothing quite as serious as this one.

On the morning of January 20, 2009 my years of experience in working with animals and my love for them wasn't enough to save me from being attacked. I walked toward my stable to feed my horses just like any other morning. The fresh dew from the grass covered the fronts of my boots as I swished across the field. The sun was just coming up. Suddenly I sensed this wasn't going to be a usual day. Just then I looked...the stable doors were open. But how had they gotten open? Perhaps, I forgot to lock them and the wind pushed them open in the middle of the night. But I never did that. I never forgot to lock my stable doors. As I stood there wondering what happened and how the doors got open the unexpected occurred. I was suddenly knocked in the back of my head with such a force that the only recollection I have is that of immediate numbness throughout my entire body. And from there my lights were out!

When I awoke, or at least when I thought I awoke, I was lying right in front of my stable where I had gotten more than the wind knocked out of me. But I really hadn't woken up at all; for I was knocked into an eight-month coma. And for each month I *thought* I was awake, I visited animals. And wouldn't you know...they could *all* talk!

1

The Stable

I looked up into the clear, blue sky or at least what I thought was a clear, blue sky for I was really fast asleep...in a rather deep sleep. I was comatose. I just didn't know it. Anyway I usually love clear, blue skies but the brightness of the clear, blue sky in the coma was just too much for my eyes. I shut them. I managed to raise myself up a bit and when I did, immediate pain shot through my neck and back. I quickly lied back down in the grass.

"Take it easy," I said to myself.

I tried opening my eyes again. Just then another sharp pain, more severe then the first traveled to my head this time. Ugh! I had a splitting headache. I looked at my watch. Nearly four hours had passed.

"This cannot be happening to me. This *cannot* be happening to me."

As I struggled to my feet I heard voices coming from inside the stable.

Thieves, I thought to myself.

I immediately lowered myself back to the ground. I mustered up enough strength to crawl over to the side of the stable where I was sure I wouldn't be seen. I dropped to the ground a few times along the way due to the pain, but I made it. Once I was there I thought to myself. I needed to find a way to get back to the house to call 911. I needed to find a way to get back to the house to retrieve my weapon. Maybe I could teach these bastards a lesson before the police came. Just then I heard their voices moving toward the stable doors. The thieves were coming out. I tried to move further back as quietly as possible away from the entrance. As I listened to them, it appeared to be the voice of a man and woman. Apparently, they were in disagreement about something. I listened closely.

"I'm not going to wait around here all day while you try to figure something out. We're free now and that's all that matters to me. I'm getting out of here whether you want to come with me or not," stated the male voice.

"But where will we go," the female voice asked. "What will we do? They'll catch us and kill us! You know that. You know the punishment for killing humans."

Killing humans? But who had they killed? The male voice spoke again and this time more indignantly:

"If you want to stay here and be charged with murder then go ahead. But I'm leaving!"

Just then I heard one horse gallop away. That's it. The thieves were stealing my horses! I listened as the female began to sob. She cried for about five minutes before taking a sudden gasp of air.

"Phyllis," she asked.

Oh my God. She was calling out my name. How had she discovered my name? I dared not answer. I dared not to even look.

"Phyllis," she asked again nervously. "Wait, Jaundis! I'm coming."

Just then I heard more galloping away. Now Jaundis was the name of my male horse. How had she discovered his name? And why was she calling it out and telling him to wait? Wait for what? The dialogue was confusing to me. To be safe, I waited until I didn't hear anything for ten minutes before making my next move. I managed to rise and shuffle myself toward the stable. I pushed the doors open. Once inside I discovered my horses were indeed gone. Stolen...at least I thought they were stolen.

Suddenly I remembered my stable phone. Ah thank goodness! A couple years ago I had the phone installed, but barely used it. Today, it would prove its worth. I walked cautiously over to the stable phone and dialed 911.

8

When the police arrived they helped me from the stable to my back porch. They then questioned me about the incident and filed a report on my missing horses. They insisted on calling the paramedics. They said my neck and head looked pretty bruised up and that I should get it checked out.

"I'm fine. Really I am," I assured them. "I have several ice packs in the fridge. Besides, the pain is wearing off now. I can move my arms and legs much better now."

"Are you sure, Dr. McClune," one of them asked. "We can have the meds here in about five minutes."

"I'm sure," I said standing up, wobbling a bit but regaining my balance. "I just really want to get inside now. I know my animals are waiting for me. I haven't been in the house since this morning."

I knew my animals were hungry. I knew they wondered what was going on with me. I could feel them. I could hear them. They were scratching against the back windows and doors, meowing, barking and tweeting while I was sitting outside with the police. Once the police left I couldn't wait to get inside. As usual all my animals were there to greet me at the door. I kneeled down to pet them. I knew they were happy to see me. I was happy to see them too, especially after what happened. However, as I reached out to pet them, to my surprise, they spoke to me quite resentfully and in plain English!

"Well, it's about time you're back," said Harper, one of my female cats. She was walking toward me slowly. "I'm absolutely starving."

I jumped to my feet in utter shock.

"What did you just say," I asked in disbelief.

"Where exactly have you been all day," asked Jackson, the other female cat now approaching me.

"What is going on around here," I asked reaching for the door knob. I prepared myself to take off running out the door in a moment.

Just then Sage, my parrot flew on to my shoulder.

"Phyllis, Phyllis, Phyllis! Feed me right now."

9

Now I was used to Sage flying onto my shoulder to greet me when I came through the door, but not speaking in English! At that moment I screamed and knocked him off of me. He then flew to the armrest of one of my chairs and clearly said: "Unbelievable." My dogs then came running up from the basement, shouting out my name requesting to be fed.

"I must be losing my mind," I said to myself.

It was the strangest thing. I could understand everything they were saying to me. At first I thought I was dreaming. Then I pinched myself. I wasn't dreaming. After feeding them and hearing them complain about the food, the amount of food and each other, I finally lied down and tried to sleep. I hoped this would all go away with a little sleep, but I couldn't due to the fact that the cats were up gossiping most of the night about what happened to me. And when I asked them to shush, they told me to shush. They said that the horses had finally got me for what I did to them and that I should be lucky to be alive, but then they said they felt sorry for me. At one point one of my dogs, Jasper even came in my bedroom and stated that he was sorry for what happened to me and told me he shouldn't have let me out that morning. He told me the night before he was snooping around the stable and heard Jaundis discussing with Tally, my female horse, what he was going to do to me. But when I spoke back, he didn't respond to me. It was as if he didn't hear what I was saying to him. It was as if I wasn't speaking to him at all. Again, I thought I was dreaming, but when I finally woke up the next *afternoon* I could still hear my animals speaking in plain English. When I opened the fish tank to feed my fishes they bellowed out: "Get well Phyllis, we love you!" At the hearing of this I spilled their food onto the floor.

"Damn it," I said.

"No problem. We'll get it up," Harper said running toward the mess. Jackson quickly joined her.

I watched as they devoured the fishes' food. Feeling helpless, I just plopped into a chair and observed them. When they were done Harper began licking her paws and complained about the fishes' food. She said: "It's just as bad

10

as our dry food...possibly even worse. Yuck!" Jackson then replied: "And here we are thinking these fish have 'the life'." Harper then said: "I suppose the grass always looks greener on the other side." They both then laughed together and walked off as if having a conversation was something they did normally.

After that incident I knew it was time for me to call someone for help. This madness had gone on long enough. Perhaps, I suffered a concussion serious enough to have an effect on how my brain processed information. I made an appointment with my physician, who also happened to be a practicing psychologist. I'd kill two birds with one stone by visiting her. I made my appointment that evening and the next day she fit me in.

"Well, the good news is nothing is broken," she said to me. "X-rays came back fine. But I do see the impact from whatever it was that hit you. I'm still not exactly sure what it could've been though. I don't know if it was an object or--"

"Jaundis," I interrupted her.

"What," she asked.

"It was Jaundis, one of my horses. He kicked me in the back of my head. I'm sure of it."

"How do you know," she asked.

"My animals told me."

At that moment she chuckled.

"I'm serious," I said getting up and putting on my jacket.

"Phyllis," she began. "Wait. I'm sorry. I just--"

"It's okay," I said. "I know it sounds crazy. But last night my cats were gossiping about what happened to me. Early this morning Jasper, my dog came in and told me they were planning it all along."

"Who was planning what all along," she asked.

I took a deep breath.

"My horses...they were planning some kind of attack on me. Or at least one of them was."

"And you say your animals told you this," she asked.

"Yes," I said timidly. "That's the other reason why I came here to see you. I've been hearing my animals speak to me for the last couple days. At first, I thought I was dreaming. I thought I was suffering from some kind of serious concussion. So I waited for whatever it was to go away, but it never did. I can hear them talking to me in plain English. I don't really know what's going on. That's really why I came to see you."

"I see," she said hesitantly. "Well, don't leave quite yet. Have a seat. Let's talk about this for a moment. What other kinds of things have you heard them say to you?"

"Everything," I began. "I can hear them say everything that comes to their minds."

"Are their lips moving when they speak to you," she asked.

"Their lips are moving," I said.

Her eyebrows rose.

"Do they tell you to do anything," she asked.

"No," I said. "They just...they just talk. They say things to me. They say things to each other. I mean, just like we're talking right now. That's how they talk."

"Do you talk back to them? Can they understand you," she asks pulling out a notepad and pen.

"I tried to...early this morning with Jasper. I tried to speak back to him, but I don't think he understood me."

"Have you tried speaking to the other animals," she asked before writing something down. Instantly, I became suspicious of her. Now maybe I shouldn't have become so suspicious, but I did.

"What are you writing down," I asked.

"I'm just taking notes," she said nonchalantly. "Have you tried talking to any of the other animals?"

"What are you going to do with the notes," I asked.

I'm an extremely private person. And if it's one thing I've learned about humans in my 52 years of being on this planet and that is you cannot completely trust them. The last thing I needed was this woman broadcasting my private business all over town. Although I trusted Doctor Lennon with my health for ten years, I had never confided in her for psychological help. What would she do with the information?

"Give me the notes," I requested.

"What," she asked.

"Give me the notes," I said firmly. "I don't want any documentation lying around here and there about what we've discussed."

"Phyllis," she said. "How long have we known each other?"

"It doesn't matter," I said.

"Let me assure you," she began. "I have a reputation in this city for keeping things confidential."

My paranoia superseded my trust.

"Give me the notes," I said again.

She chuckled. Then she looked down at the notes and back up at me. She realized I was serious.

"Fine," she said ripping them out of the notebook and handing them to me.

"You'll tell no one of this," I said getting up and leaving out. I left abruptly from her office and never returned.

Before I returned home that afternoon I decided to change the menu up a bit for my animals. I remembered their complaints. I wanted to see what would happen if I gave them something different. I was limited as to what I could get for Sage and the fish, but for my cats and dogs I bought fresh fish and chicken. After all, they were carnivorous creatures. I cut up some vegetables into tiny pieces, sautéed them and added them to some cooked meat before seasoning the whole batch. It smelled so good I actually had a bowl myself.

After a few sniffs, the dogs dove right into their bowls. However, the cats were quite suspicious.

"What is this," Harper asked smelling the new food.

"I don't know, but the smell is overwhelmingly good," said Jackson.

"Well then shall we try it," asked Harper.

"You first," said Jackson.

Harper licked the food several times before taking a rather large chunk into her teeth.

"It's delicious," she said chomping. "It's absolutely delicious! It's real food."

"Well of course it's real food you idiot," said Jackson. "What else would it be?"

"No," said Harper. "I mean it's *real food.*"

As I stood there watching my animals happily devour their meal, the only concern I had was that now they would no longer eat their dry, old food. I would be stuck cooking for them and myself each day from here on out.

That evening I retrieved the notes from Doctor Lennon and threw them into the fireplace. I watched them burn. Sage came and landed gently on my shoulder. It'd been a few days since he'd done that. I suppose he was a bit disgruntled about me knocking him off days ago.

"I'm sorry," I said to him.

2

The Shelter

In the following month I couldn't believe no one reported seeing any missing horses. I thought surely I would have had them back by now. After all, I was the only person in the area with two missing Yellow Rose Arabian horses. I was sure of that. It was time to conduct a more serious search for them. If I was going to get them back it would be because I worked hard to get them back my self. I began by visiting the local shelter. I frequented the shelter to treat animals, but it was also where I'd acquired my own.

"Dr. McClune...long time, no see," joyfully shouted Steve, the manager of the shelter. His friendliness could be a bit annoying at times, but overall he was a nice, young fellow. He rose out of his seat to greet me. Although I'd shared with Steve countless times how unnecessary it was to get up from his seat for me, he insisted on doing so. About three years ago, Steve and I had an in-depth conversation about animals' connection to humans. He was fascinated with the knowledge I shared with him and developed quite a strange liking for me afterwards. He jokingly began calling me "Misses Dr. Do-Little" and had a terrible habit of greeting me loudly as soon as I walked through the door as if he were making some sort of special announcement. Perhaps, I should have been flattered by all of this, but it was quite irritating at times.

"How are you," he asked shaking my hand.

"Fine, fine," I said.

"I haven't seen or heard from you in quite a while, doctor," he said. "I have some animals that really need to see you."

"Yes, well I've been busy," I lied. I hadn't been busy at all. I'd been preoccupied with losing my mind, hearing animals talk and what not. .

"Well, it's always a pleasure to see you, doctor," he said excitedly. "What animals will you see today?"

I chuckled.

"I'm actually here for a different reason this time, Steve," I said removing my backpack from my shoulders. I took out the flyers I'd put together the night before and handed him two of them. "My horses are missing."

He gasped. "Your horses are missing?"

"Yes," I began. "They're Yellow Rose--"

"Arabian horses," he finished my sentence looking down at the pictures on the flyers. "They're beautiful."

"Yes," I said. "They've been missing for...going on two months now.

"Wow," he exclaimed scratching his forehead.

"I know. It's been a while. I was just trying to give them time to return," I explained. "I thought surely someone would've seen them by now and reported them to the police."

"I don't think so, Dr. McClune," he chuckled. "These are quite expensive horses. And you know how people are these days. They'll just catch them and sell them."

I didn't want to think about someone catching Jaundis and Tally and putting them up for sale. I changed the subject.

"Actually, I was wondering if I could take a look in the shelter's stables before I left."

"Oh, we haven't gotten any horses in, in a while," he said.

I could feel myself growing impatient with him.

"I'd just like to take a quick look," I said a little rudely.

"Alright...sure," he said looking at me oddly. "No problem. Let me just put these flyers up for you real quick, grab my jacket and we can head on back."

As we walked through the halls of the shelter toward the stables, I could not believe my ears. I could not believe what I heard coming from inside the animals' rooms. The cats and dogs were all calling for me.

"Dr. McClune," they all shouted, but not in unison.

16

It startled me at first...to hear so many of them calling out my name at once. For a moment, I stopped in the middle of the hallway. Then I noticed it wasn't only my name they were shouting out. Some of the dogs were demanding to be walked or fed. Many of the cats wanted their pans cleaned and some of them wanted to be walked as well. The fact that some cats wanted to be walked was a bit surprising. I heard one dog say: "Clean my cage." And another one said: "Everybody shut up! I'm trying to sleep." I heard a few of the cats through the walls shouting out: "Take me home, Dr. McClune!" But another one said: "Why would anyone want to take you home? The only thing you're going to do is vomit all over everything!" I even heard one of the dogs shout out that she was in excruciating pain and that she was too young to die.

"Is everything alright in here," I asked Steve concerned.

"Well, yeah," he replied. "Why wouldn't it be?"

Obviously he wasn't hearing what I was hearing. Things couldn't have been alright in here. It was unbelievable how many of the animals claimed to be in a state of emergency. Their cries seemed to grow louder and louder each moment. I closed my eyes, placed my fingers inside my ears and began to hum.

"Dr. McClune," said Steve.

I didn't hear him for humming so loudly.

"Dr. McClune," he said again. He tapped me slightly on my arm. I lost it.

"Shut up, shut up, and shut up! All of you just shut up and leave me alone," I screamed out at the animals.

I didn't mean to scare them, but just like that they all went completely silent. When I opened my eyes Steve was standing a few feet from me with his arms crossed. His eyebrows were raised and he looked nearly afraid. I regained my composure.

"I'm terribly sorry," I said. "I just...I've become very sensitive to noise."

"It's okay," he said. "So...if you just follow these arrows they'll point you right into the stables. I think I'm just going to go on back to the office now. Um...I've got some calls to return anyway."

I made him uneasy.

"Sure," I said now embarrassed.

"If you need me, just uh....," he swallowed. "You can push the red button on the wall, near the entrance of the stable and I'll be there in a moment. Okay?"

"Yeah, sure," I said.

I watched him quickly return to his office.

I'd really done it this time. My good reputation was officially in the process of destruction. What was going on with me? What was happening inside of me? As much as Steve annoyed me, I'd never treated him with such discourtesy. I'd never displayed any hostility toward animals and certainly not with someone looking on. Before the accident I was well respected, but now I was giving people a reason to label me insane. It wouldn't be long now before I was known as the Town Quack instead of the Town Vet.

As I entered the shelter's stable, the doors shut rather quickly behind me. For a moment I looked around. Ugh! The smell was atrocious. I had been in here several times before to treat horses, but this time, in the coma...the smell was absolutely terrible. Luckily I kept a handkerchief in my back pocket. I retrieved it to cover my face. It was dark and rather creepy as well.

"Well, if it isn't Misses Dr. Do-Little herself," a deep voice said from behind. There was laughter, neighing and stomping from the horses throughout the stable at this saying.

I quickly turned around to see where the voice was coming from, but I didn't see anyone.

"Over here," the same voice said.

I looked to my right and out of the darkness a large, white horse appeared. He was standing in the corner of his stall lapping up water from a small bucket.

"Looking for Jaundis and Tally, I presume," he said now fixing his eyes on me.

"Yes, I am," I said walking toward his stall. "How did you know that? Do you know where they are? Do you know where I can find them?"

"Maybe I do...maybe I don't," he said. It was so dark I could barely see his face. He stood in the back and refused to come forward.

"You can understand what I'm saying," I asked.

"Of course I can understand you," he said. "I'm 42 years old. I've been around humans all my life. I understand everything they're saying. Sometimes they don't have to say anything at all and I can still understand them."

"Can you please tell me where I can find Jaundis and Tally," I asked.

"I wouldn't tell you if I did," he said.

"Please," I said nearly in tears. "Don't you see I'm desperate? You said you understand humans. Then you can understand how desperate I am right now. Please, please help me! Please tell me where they are."

"Oh woman," he began. "Get a hold of yourself. I'll tell you where they are."

"Oh good," I said.

"Once we discuss what's in it for me," he added.

"What do you mean," I asked.

"What's in it for me? What am I going to get out of this...sharing this pertinent information with you? What are you going to do for me, Dr. Phyllis McClune?"

"I don't know," I said. "What do you want?"

He then began walking towards me, but very slowly.

"Well, you see," he began. "My previous owner...he was an old man. He raised me from a foal and named me Clement. But one day while he was brushing me he suffered a terrible stroke. I tried to revive him by stomping on his chest several times. But it was just...no...use. He was already dead. About a week later humans finally arrived and took him away. Then more humans arrived and took everything from the house, including me. But you see, no one wanted to keep me because of this spot on the side of my ass."

19

He turned to his right side so I could view it. It was a medium-sized grey spot. It was about the size of an average hand.

"That's when I got shuffled off to this shelter. See, my previous owner never mentioned this spot. To be honest, I didn't even know I had it. But these people...these people who come in here everyday, looking for a God-damned horse, they say: "Look at the white horse. Look at the beautiful, white horse." And then they ask for a closer look. And when they get a closer look they see my spot. And then they ask: "Do you have any other white horses? Do you have any other *all* white horses?" So I've been here for about five years now facing rejection after rejection after rejection due to this spot on the side of my ass. Five years of: "turn to the left now turn to the right...uh-oh." And my patience, dear Misses Dr. Do-Little has just about run out. So...what can you do for me, you ask. What can Misses Dr. Do-Little do for me?"

He then charged at me and crashed into the door of his compartment. It startled me. I took several steps back. He did it on purpose. I knew it because he began laughing after the fact. The other horses throughout the stalls joined in the laughter, but it wasn't funny to me at all.

"Do an old boy a favor, won't you doctor," he said. "It gets a little cramped inside here sometimes. Release me from this prison!"

"I'm sorry for what you've had to experience, Clement," I said sympathetically. "But at the moment I'm not looking for a third horse. I'm looking for the two I lost."

"Don't flatter your self, doctor," he said. "I'm not looking for you to make room for me. I want to be released into the wild!"

"Absolutely out of the question," I retorted.

"Then I guess you'll never see your Jaundis and Tally again," he said huffily.

"You don't understand...I could go to jail," I said. "I could...I could lose my license!"

Just then he turned around and walked slowly to the back of his stall. I listened as he began lapping up water again. I thought about Jaundis and Tally. I thought about the

20

risk. I wanted to see my horses so badly it was becoming unbearable.

"Alright," I said. "I'll do it. Now just tell me where they are!"

He looked up at me.

"Not so fast, my lady," he said walking toward me again. "How do I know you'll keep your word? Humans cannot be trusted."

"I'll come back," I said.

"When," he asked.

"I can't say when. But you must give me time to think things out. I'll come back to set you free...I promise."

"But what about my friends," he asked as if he were making a suggestion.

"No Clement! This deal is between you and me," I said.

"Then we don't have a deal at all," he said walking away.

"What," I said.

"We don't have a deal," he yelled. "You can't just free me and not the others."

"This is insane," I said. "Where are you all going to go? What are you going to do once you get there?"

"That's none of your concern," he said. "Now do we have a deal or don't we, because I have to catch up on my afternoon naps."

"Damn you," I said. "Alright, fine! I'll free you...and your friends. Now tell me where I can find Jaundis and Tally."

He looked into my eyes for a moment as if he were trying to read me. It was as if he was trying to read my mind.

"You'll find them near State Street and Michigan Avenue, downtown," he said.

I laughed.

"You're a liar," I said.

"No," he said. "Lying is a human trait. Animals...we don't lie. We have no reason to. We hold no hidden motives. The truth is...Jaundis and Tally were found some time ago. The humans that caught them were dishonest and instead of turning them in like they should've, they used them to gain money. Now they're pulling homo-sapiens around in coaches."

At the hearing of this news my heart sank into my chest. The idea of my beautiful horses being forced to pull humans around infuriated me. It was as if I'd been knocked in the back of the head again.

As I made my exit Clement spoke to me one last time.

"And doctor," he said. "Just so you know...whether you decide to return here and free us or not...I'm going to bust out of this place. And when I do the first place I'll visit is the one that belongs to you."

I couldn't wait to get out of that stable. As soon as I did, I took a deep breath of fresh air. I then heard the horses laughing and stomping on the stable floor. They made a most thunderous sound.

Remembering the terrible smell of horse feces in the shelter's stable encouraged me to be more responsible about my own animals' waste. I went to empty Harper and Jackson's litter boxes as soon as I came home.

"What has gotten into her lately," Harper asked sniffing into the air.

"I don't know," said Jackson. "But whatever it is...I'm starting to like it."

Nothing had gotten into me. I just realized how I would feel if I made a bowel movement somewhere and a few hours later I returned to find it still there; or if I had to return to make a new bowel movement in the same place as the old one. I thought about how I would feel if I accidentally stepped in it and how it might feel to be surrounded by waste. In the future, I would invest some time in training my cats how to use it somewhere else; perhaps outside, in the same manner as my dogs.

3

The City

Along with losing my mind I was losing track of time. My horses had been missing for nearly three months before I finally decided to visit State Street and Michigan Avenue, located downtown, where Clement said I would find them. And find them, I did. There they were standing side-by-side, right on the corner, strapped and saddled. It hurt me to see them like that, but I calmed myself and walked quickly over to them...so quickly I didn't see the stray cat sitting in my path. I accidentally stepped on its tail.

"Hey," it screamed out. "Watch where you're going ass wipe!"

"I'm terribly sorry," I said.

But I was in a hurry.

"Jaundis, Tally," I shouted walking toward them again.

Tally raised her head.

"Phyllis," she asked.

I walked right up to both of them. At that moment, I was so happy to see them I didn't care who saw me talking to them.

"Tally," I said embracing her.

"Oh Phyllis," said Tally. "You're alive! You're alive!"

"Of course I'm alive," I said looking into her eyes.

"Oh, I'm so happy to see you. I'm so relieved," she said. "Phyllis, please forgive me...please forgive us! I'm so sorry for everything."

"It's okay," I said with tears now forming in my eyes. "I'm just so happy to see you both, really I am!"

I then reached out to touch Jaundis, but when I did, he pulled his head back away from me.

"Jaundis," I said.

He didn't respond.

"Jaundis," I said again wiping my tears away.

"Don't worry about him," said Tally. "He's still upset that's all."

"Upset about what," I asked turning to him. "What are you upset about?"

He ignored me.

"I've come to get you both out of here," I said. "That's what I've come to do. I brought the purchase papers with me. I'm going to call the police right now. We're going home."

"Leave us," Jaundis then spoke angrily.

"What," I asked. "Do you want to be here?"

"Yes," he said.

I was shocked. Then I remembered what my cats said about the accident. I thought about what Jasper, my dog revealed to me about Jaundis.

"It's true isn't it? You attacked me, didn't you?"

He didn't speak.

"I thought we were a happy family," I said.

"You thought," he snapped. "That's the problem with you humans. You think you know so much about us."

"Can you tell me what I've done wrong," I asked.

"Where do I begin," he asked. "Let's start with the castration. Let's move on to the branding. Let's continue with the constant cutting and snipping and the being locked up inside the stable all day long while you're busy, out treating all the other animals in the world that need to be treated besides your own."

"Jaundis," Tally said.

"What? You're too afraid to speak up for yourself and now you want to stop me from speaking up for myself as well? She wants to know why we're out here, so I'm going to tell her why. I'm going to tell her why we'd rather be out here than to be with her. The famous Dr. Phyllis McClune! The real Dr. Do-Little! Oh how nice it must be to be owned by such a woman, they say. Oh you must have the life, Jaundis! Oh you must be so happy, Jaundis! That's what the other

24

horses say to me. But little do they know how truly neglectful you are, Phyllis McClune. We may be pulling humans around for a living but at least we have respect. We receive admiration from people we don't even know. We're thoroughly washed each day in warm water *and* soap. We return to clean stalls at night and are given fresh fruits and vegetables in the morning. Unlike you seem to believe, our new owner understands the importance of paying attention to his animals. He knows no one wants to be around smelly, dirty horses especially when they go all around the city. His goal is to maintain the best, most expensive horse buggy business in town and he knows that depends on having the best horses so we're all treated well with the utmost respect. We have a good diet; we get proper sleep and hourly exercise. So the answer to your question is yes, Dr. McClune...we *want* to be here!"

I was taken back. I looked into his eyes and then into Tally's.

"Does he speak for you too," I asked her.

She looked at him.

"Does he speak for you," I said again firmly.

"Well," she began

"Excuse me ma'am." Just then a man approached me in a bright, red suit with a large top hat on. I assumed he was the coachman.

"I'm sorry," he said. "I had to stop for an emergency bathroom break. Can I interest you in a tour of the city?"

"No thank you," I said.

"Are you sure," he asked boarding the coach. "This happens to be one of our best coaches."

"No thank you," I said again.

"Very well, then," he said. "I must be off now. Have a good day. Yah!"

I placed my hand over my mouth to keep from screaming. There I watched as my horses trotted off with a complete stranger, but there was nothing I could do for them. They didn't want me to do anything for them.

That night I went to bed absolutely stunned. Jaundis' words permeated through my brain. I tried to make sense of it all. I couldn't believe he felt that way about me. I didn't know I was treating them so badly. Truth is, I didn't believe what my cats said the night of the attack. I doubted what Jasper told me about it that morning. I just knew when I got to State Street and Michigan Avenue my horses would be just as happy to see me as I was to see them. But I was sadly mistaken...very sadly mistaken.

4

The Zoo

In the following month I purposed it in my heart to forget about Jaundis and Tally. Thinking of them only seemed to depress me. In fact, I desired to forget about horses altogether. I also had become annoyed with domesticated animals, mainly cats and dogs. With my new ability to understand their speech, I learned of their humanness and they complained far too much for me. So when I returned to treating animals I decided to work with exotic animals instead at the zoo. Besides, I was sure the news of my pending insanity hadn't yet spread to the zookeepers.

I turned to the zoo for some relief and in part, I got it. For one, zoo animals didn't speak as much because most times they were heavily sedated. Before the animals got too instinctive you see, part of my job was to assist in keeping them calm by issuing medication to them by injection or in the form of "vitamins." Animals' instincts were powerful and highly unpredictable. The vitamins aided in keeping them more predictable and under control; they settled them. They were able to do anything and everything one could possibly imagine. In fact, however we wanted the animals to feel or not feel, whatever we wanted them to do or not do, we had the power to make it happen by medication. It worked like magic. But for me, it became quite depressing after a while. The lions spent most of their time sleeping, not because they were naturally tired, but because they were medicated to remain calm; tiredness was simply a side-effect. It may have seemed harsh, but if the lions' instincts weren't depressed they would behave like the animals they were and possibly startle the visiting patrons. If the gorillas and monkeys weren't given hyper-active medication, they could easily become depressed for various reasons and even speak of committing suicide. If the rattlesnakes were not induced with what we called "friendly" vitamins, they would strike out at the visiting patrons continuously. Believe it or not, even the dolphins had the potential to turn malicious without their daily dose. The elephants were highly aggressive animals as well. And if they missed one dose of their medication, which was a rather large dose by the way, they would attack everything and everyone in sight. The vitamins also aided in population control and assured us we wouldn't have more animals than space to put them all in. We even had vitamins that could control hunger and thirst.

Thinking of all this, I couldn't imagine how it must've been for veterinarians during the first round of animal importation to zoos. This was a time before humans discovered ways to control animals by medication of course; a time when animals were being controlled more physically rather than mentally. Before I could understand animals' speech, I have to admit, I was unconcerned with how we controlled them. But in my coma, I began to wonder to what extent we should control animals at all, and especially by chemical substances. I was beginning to see the importance of leaving animals in their own natural environments and allowing nature to do the rest. But for these zoo animals, which were now several generations from being left in their natural environments, wasn't it far too late to put them back? If we took these zoo animals and placed them back in their environments wouldn't it prove disastrous? Would they be able to even survive? For these animals, their natural environments are no longer their natural environments anymore than Africa is home to the entire human race. Some of their natural environments have been destroyed, leaving the zoos their only means to continue life. Have these animals become totally dependent on us and the medication we prescribe for them, which could also be altering their DNA? Damn it! We should've left them alone to begin with. At the most, we should've organized wildlife reserves for them. Oh how have we allowed our capitalism to destroy the very things that should remain natural to us?

28

In a few weeks, needless to say, I quit working at the zoo. It became overwhelming for me. I handed in my letter of resignation, but it was hardly taken seriously. The zookeepers were astonished at my radical statements. I told them the monkeys were suicidal. Instead of taking me seriously, they made mockery of what I wrote and spread the news that "Misses Dr. Do-Little" was indeed off her rocker.

That evening upon returning home, I took my dogs for a walk. And this time, I did something different. For the very first time, I took Harper and Jackson outside for a walk too. I wanted them to smell the fresh air. I wanted them to experience the night sky. But they spent most of their first time outside being afraid. And when the neighbors saw me walking my cats, they stared at me. The news of my madness had spread to them. Walking my cats would serve as a little proof that the rumors were true. Yes, this would be enough to officially put me on the radar.

5

The Human Pet

In the fifth month I arose in my coma as a canine...a bull dog to be exact. And for some unknown reason I hated everyone except for my owner, whom everyone called Buster. I especially hated other dogs. When I saw them I yelled out obscenities at them and dared them to mess with me. When I did get the opportunity to fight them I tore them from limb to limb each time. I had a reputation for winning all my fights. Buster was proud of me for it. I was his trophy. He'd trained me to be the Mike Tyson of Dog Fighting on my block. I was known as the Dog Killer and I wore that title proudly. It worked like this. A couple days before the fights Buster wouldn't feed me so when I got into the ring with my opponents I was literally blood thirsty. When I won the fights Buster always rewarded me with a big, fat, juicy steak! Now I had never been afraid of fighting before, but when I stepped into the ring with a pit bull named Husky I began to doubt my self. Husky was much larger than I was. He was strong and I could smell he was just as blood thirsty as I was. When I displayed some reluctance to enter the fighting pen, my owner screamed at me:

"Get in there, you stupid bitch!" he said angrily.

For the first time I'd embarrassed him in front of his friends. Even if I won the fight I could expect a beating when I got home for showing fear. Just then Husky thrust himself into me. He slashed me across my face with his sharpened claws. Blood fell from my face onto the ground. I licked it. I had never tasted my own blood before. It tasted rather good. It distracted me though. Before I knew it Husky slashed at me again and this time he bit down hard into my neck. Now my

30

neck was bleeding. Soon I became dizzy. I fell flat on my side.

"Get up, get up!" I heard Buster shout.

I tried to, but I couldn't. I just couldn't. I let him down. I knew it. I was losing blood fast and as a result, I lost all strength. I could hardly even blink my eyes. Husky had won, but he wasn't done with me yet. He walked over to me, reached down and took my neck into his mouth. He then lifted me off the ground. He threw me into it one last time before I closed my eyes and died.

When I opened my eyes again I was as light as a feather and standing on a branch. I thought I was in heaven but then I looked to my sides and I had dark, feathered wings. Then I looked down and I had some strange looking feet. I was a bird. That meant I could fly! And when I realized I could fly I took off. At first, I couldn't believe how easy it was to do it. Surely there must be something else to it. I flew everywhere I thought to before I remembered I was pregnant and needed to build a nest for my offspring. So I waited until the sun came up, sang for about an hour or two and then went off searching for the best materials to build a strong and sturdy nest. But on my way to pick up a fallen twig I heard a loud blast. A few seconds later I felt severe pain on my backside. It was absolutely unbearable pain. I plummeted to the ground. And the last thing I saw was a man's hand reaching out for my face.

When I awoke again I was swimming in water, but not like a fish in the ocean. I was swimming very slowly; for I was very large. I looked down at myself. I immediately identified myself as a Manatee. I came to the surface to breath in some air before going back down to the bottom of my aquarium. I wanted to finish looking at the humans through the glass below before my show began. I was just as curious about them as they were me. My trainers taught me to wave at them with my front flippers. So I did. The humans always waved back at me. And when they waved I was supposed to wave back at them again and again. They always laughed at this. Then the music began to play. I got excited. I was trained to do all sorts of things when I heard *A Hard Day's Night* by the Beatles played then whistled by my trainers. Oh I twisted and spun. I burst into speeds up to fifteen miles an hour and dove to the bottom of the tank before pushing my self up again to the surface! The crowd always went wild at this.

"Dance!" they shouted.

The more applause I received the more treats I received afterwards. Yes, I was having a good old time. I was having a great time right before I closed my eyes and awakened as a spider!

I looked and counted...1...2...3...4...5...6...7...8 legs! It was confirmed. I was a spider. I didn't care for spiders. How had I become one? My instincts kicked in. I had several eggs to lay. It was time for me to find a place to build a secure web for them. When I found a place, it was a nice corner behind a door. *No one would spot us here*, I thought. There I took my time and built a very nice web for my babies. I then waited patiently to lay them. While I was waiting I heard a human say:

"What about these cobwebs?"

"Yes, I know," said another human. "Apparently, the custodial staff isn't quite doing their job."

Oh no. I knew I would have to find a more secure place. When the door closed humans might spot me after all. So I went searching for another corner. I tried to move as quickly as possible without being seen. I discovered an area behind the trash can. It seemed secure. This may be a wonderful spot, but I couldn't think too much about it because I could feel my eggs. They were ready to come out. I decided to start weaving. Besides, the trash can was large. I figured it would take time to fill it up. By the time it was full and the humans thought to move it, I would've already had my babies and be moving on with my life.

In the next few hours I laid about one hundred eggs on my new web. I then began wrapping them in nice, silk sacs. I worked very hard to make sure they were nice and secure. Then it happened. The most preposterous thing took place. The custodial staff removed the trash can from its place,

32

tearing my web. I ran as fast as I could but it was no use. My eggs and I were smashed by a hot, wet, *bleached* rag!

6

Wolf

In the sixth month, I arose as a wolf. It was the most frightening thing of all...even for someone comatose. I felt weird for some reason, and so, I immediately jumped out of the hospital bed. Much to my surprise, I landed on my very own hind legs, yet I stood completely upright as any human being. I looked down at all the hair and fur and could not believe what I was seeing. I had paws for hands and claws for nails. I could barely close my mouth because my teeth were suddenly very long and sharp.

I walked slowly over to the mirror across from my bed, attempting to touch my hairy face, but I had trouble because my front legs wouldn't bend. I couldn't believe what I was seeing and so I intended to scream at the top of my lungs, but only a howl came out.

Before the door of my hospital room even opened I sensed someone was near. So, I ran and hid behind some curtains in the room, near the window.

"Excuse me, are you alright, madam," the soft voice asked, entering inside and sounding concerned.

"Fine," I replied surprised that I could talk.

That was shocking. I could talk. In fact, it was my very own voice. "Fine," I said again.

"Good. Then, do you mind coming out from behind that curtain? It's meal time," the voice said.

I could barely see the face of the person who was speaking, but it sounded like a woman's voice. It was rather soft and pleasant. It put me at ease. I could simply tell her that I didn't know what was going on and that I didn't know why I had a wolf's body. I could try to convince her not to scream or run…that I was harmless and wouldn't eat her. So, I took a deep breath and pushed the curtain back only to reveal the most hideous thing of all standing right in front of me…another wolf, only dressed as a nurse.

Before I could even think of what to do, my body reacted to the fear of unexpectedly seeing a wolf dressed as a nurse. I turned and burst through the hospital window, shattering glass everywhere. And when I landed, I did so nearly four stories below…right on my feet! And when I landed, I looked and wolves were everywhere! Wolves walking down the street holding hands and kissing, wolves with wolf babies, wolves driving, wolf policemen…wolves, wolves, wolves! Wolves every where acting like humans, dressing like humans! I took off running at an unimaginable speed.

As a human, I was lucky to run five minutes straight without feeling as if I were in need of an oxygen tank, but as a wolf, I ran nearly twenty minutes straight and still had air in my lungs.

I found myself in a dark alley. That's where I realized I could smell and hear everything. The slightest movement caught my eye and gained my suspicion.

Then, without warning, came this insatiable appetite…for meat and blood. I needed it. I needed it now. Suddenly the wolf nurse's words echoed through my head.

"…it's meal time," I remember her saying.

Yes, it was meal time. Why had I run off right when it was meal time?!? How stupid of me! At least, I could have eaten. At that moment, I looked up and there, standing all alone, on a street corner, all by itself, just happened to be…a meat shop! What luck!

"Ah ha," I exclaimed.

As I walked briskly to the meat shop, forgetting that I had not even a single dime to my name to buy anything, I was stared at by other passer-by wolves walking in the street and driving in their cars. I guess they weren't used to seeing a wolf half-dressed in a hospital gown scooting across the street in broad daylight. Just then the wind blew my gown

35

slightly open revealing my wolf ass. I watched as a mother-wolf quickly covered her kid-wolf's eyes.

"It ain't nothin' he ain't already seen wolf lady," I said sarcastically.

She gasped at me as I walked by her and kid-wolf, entering the meat shop.

The truth is, I could smell the meat shop nearly two miles away before arriving inside. My mouth began to water.

"Can...can I help you," the wolf salesperson said, standing behind the counter looking puzzled at me.

"What's the matter," I asked drooling now at the sight of all the meat in the glass counter. "Never seen a hungry wolf in a hospital gown before?"

I had never seen such meat in all my life...human meat; still soaked and covered in blood...mmm. Now, any other time I would be absolutely disgusted by this savagely cruel display, but as a hungry wolf, it was exactly what I needed: an overabundance of human meat right before my very eyes in all assortments, I tell you; hands, arms, legs, thighs, and breasts! It was any wolf's dream. Organized so perfectly for any hungry wolf to pick out exactly what she wanted for dinner tonight.

"I'll have three legs, two thighs, a tongue, and an arm," I said anxiously, not believing what was coming out of my own mouth. Here I was standing in a human meat shop requesting human body parts to eat.

"And a few of those baby necks too," I said.

The wolf salesperson looked at me strangely.

"That's fine, ma'am," he began. "But if you'll kindly get a ticket and wait in line like everyone else, then I'll be happy to serve you."

That would have been fine, except for, as a wolf, my temper and hunger were two things I couldn't control. Before I knew it, I'd hopped on top of the counter and began beating it in violently with my claws and face.

"Stop it, stop it," one of the wolf customers screamed.

"Grab her, she's crazy," another one said.

"Watch out," I heard one of them yell.

36

"I'm calling the cops," screamed the wolf salesperson.

"I'm hungry now," I screamed and continued bashing in walls and clawing at anything in sight.

Just then two wolf policeman entered and fought me. We scratched and clawed at each other until they finally wrestled me to the ground and placed me in handcuffs. I was taken away to the squad car kicking and howling. It took at least five of them to hold me down.

"I'm just hungry...Jesus Christ!" I screamed.

Once inside the squad car, I stared out the window still hungry, but now angry more than ever.

Just then a stranger wolf ran up to the squad car, beat on the window and said to me:

"Don't worry. I got it all on tape!"

7

The Escape

In the seventh month, near the end of my coma, I sensed I was lying in my bed again. I was afraid to open my eyes though. I was afraid I was another animal, maybe a cow off to the slaughter house or something like that. So before I opened my eyes I felt for my legs and arms. Then I peeked open one of my eyes and recognized my two feet. I let out a sigh of relief. I was myself again.

It was a beautiful morning. The sun shone brightly through my windows. I got up to make myself some coffee. I cooked fresh eggs and ham, divided it between myself and my animals and together we ate heartily. As usual, they devoured each slice of meat. But as I looked at them, something was different about them. Then it came to me. I hadn't heard any of them say one word. I waited for them to comment on the breakfast, but even after breakfast, they never said one word. I watched as my cats walked off side-by-side saying absolutely nothing to each other. What was going on? I picked up Harper.

"Say something. Say something to me," I said to her.

But she said absolutely nothing. She just looked at me. I burst into laughter. I was regaining my sanity!

At that moment I wanted to call everyone in my neighborhood and tell them I wasn't crazy after all. I wanted to call Doctor Lennon and tell her I was cured. I wanted to call the zoo and tell them maybe I was wrong about the monkeys. I paced the floor. I was so excited I turned on the T.V. Now I never turned on the T.V., but when I did the news came on. A special report was being given on some animals that had escaped from the town shelter:

38

"This just in...Twenty-three horses escaped from the Schaumburg Shelter around one o'clock this morning. Sources say although there was no sign of forced entry there was definitely a sign of a forced exit. Our Nina Johnson is there reporting at the scene. Nina?"

"Yes, I'm here Bill. I'm standing here with Steve Cox, the manager of the Schaumburg Shelter. Steve, can you tell us what happened here?"

"Well I came in this morning and..."

Everything else he said was a blur because I suddenly remembered Clement. A few months ago I'd promised him I would return to free him and his friends from the shelter. I'd completely forgotten! Then his words came back to me: *"And just so you know...whether you decide to return here and free us or not...I'm going to bust out of this place. And when I do the first place I'll visit is the one that belongs to you."*

Just then I heard galloping around the house. I quickly arose to retrieve my gun from my bedroom closet. Now usually I wouldn't think of harming an animal, but Clement was no ordinary animal. Thank goodness my gun was already loaded. I cocked it back. At that moment I heard glass shattering in the living room. It was Clement. Just that quick he'd crashed through my glass, balcony doors and was making his way to my bedroom. I turned around slowly. He was already standing there in my bedroom doorway.

"Clement," I said.

Without warning he charged at me full force. I tried to point the gun at him and fire, but he was too quick. He knocked the gun completely out of my hands and ran right into me. My back hit hard up against the closet door. I reeled to the ground helplessly. I shook my self. When I opened my eyes Clement was standing right over me.

"Perhaps Jaundis failed in his attempt to kill you, my dear Phyllis...but I certainly will not!"

Then he gathered all the strength in his body and used his legs to stomp my lights out yet again!

8

The Awakening

When I woke up...I mean when I really woke up from my coma nearly eight months later, I didn't believe I was awake. In fact, a few weeks past before I believed I was truly awake; for in my coma, I'd waken up multiple times and I wasn't truly awake. But this time...this time I was truly awakened.

When the news spread that I was up, in the following days, my hospital room filled quickly with family and friends. It was odd because a few of them I'd just seen in my coma: Steve, several of my neighbors, some of the zookeepers who made mockery of me. They all brought me flowers and balloons. Having all this attention really was quite overwhelming for me though. There I was lying there without a proper bath in months and guests filing in. I tried to be nice while they were there, but after they were gone, I requested not to have anymore visitors.

Unbeknownst to me, Doctor Lennon had been my main caretaker while I was at the hospital. She made sure I was well tended to and was by my side when I was informed I was paralyzed from the waste down. I'd already sensed that. Before they broke the news to me, I'd tried to move my legs several times and couldn't do it.

"You were robbed," Doctor Lennon said. "They hit you in the back of the head with a steel pole. But they didn't get very far. The police caught them and took them right to jail."

So I hadn't been attacked by my horses after all. It was a relief. It had all been a complete nightmare. Furthermore, I was informed that friends and family took turns caring for my animals and home while I was away. Whenever I was ready to return home all my animals would be there waiting for me.

Although I wanted to go home and tend to them right away I couldn't. If I went home now I knew I would be calling on people here and there to assist me. When I returned home I wanted to be on my own. So I made the conscious decision to get therapy first. In the following months I was moved to a rehabilitation center where I could focus on regaining strength, particularly in my upper body. I also learned how to move around in a wheelchair. It was most difficult. When my sister saw me struggling she insisted I get an electric wheelchair, but I knew if I got one my arms wouldn't get the exercise they needed.

"Just let me make my own decisions," I snapped at her.

I appreciated Katherine, my younger sister, truly I did. I appreciated everyone that was trying to help me, but I just got frustrated at times with some of them. I was paralyzed, not anesthetized. I couldn't use my legs, but I could still use my brain. Now that I was awake, I didn't need anyone making any decisions for me. I enjoyed having independence. I wanted to do things on my own. I was bitterly angry about losing the motion in my legs. I was completely saddened by it. I thought about the hyper-active medication I issued to monkeys in my coma and thought about getting some in reality for myself. It was hard enough to have to deal with my new handicap, let alone having to get used to people assisting me with the simplest tasks. It wasn't a big deal for them, but it was for me.

In the third month of my rehabilitation it was evident my hard work was paying off. I could lift myself from the bed into the wheelchair on my very own. I learned how to shower, dress myself and even go for a stroll, literally on my own. About four months later I felt I was ready to go home.

"Are you sure," Katherine asked.

"Yes," I said growing impatient with her.

"And if you need anything or help doing something promise me you will call for help."

At first I didn't respond to her.

"Phyllis," she said sounding like our mother.

"Alright, alright, I will," I said reluctantly. "Just take me home."

I missed my animals more than ever. It had been nearly a year since I saw them. I was anxious to get home and anxious to get back to work in whatever capacity I could. Before arriving though I knew I needed to do a few more things. I needed to prepare my home. I was handicapped now. I wanted to make sure I could get around on my own and still care for my animals as much as possible. So I installed a fence that rendered me a very large backyard. The animals would be able to run around freely. I also wouldn't have to walk them or depend on anyone to do it for me. It would be much easier for me to simply let them out. I also installed lifts to assist me in getting from one place to the other in my wheelchair. The third thing I did was reluctantly hire an assistant to help me with my horses throughout the week. This way I ensured the horses got proper care at least until I learned how to do it on my own.

I decided to return home in the spring. Other than the fact that some of my fish were now dead, all of my other animals were intact. Jasper and the dogs clobbered me at the door. Harper and Jackson were there too sniffing around my wheelchair, licking my feet and legs. I lifted them up and placed them gently on my lap. Sage flew onto the arm of my chair and began chirping. I burst into laughter as I remembered how they greeted me in the coma.

Being in a wheelchair, I had to remember to be extra careful around so many tails. I rolled myself out to the stable for the first time. I stopped and looked around in the place where I was attacked...in the same place where I'd been knocked down. I took a deep breath. I was knocked into a coma and remembered everything that happened in it; nearly every detail. I thought to myself. Perhaps I wouldn't be able to start a revolution about how animals were treated from my artificial experience, but I could revolutionize myself. I rolled into the stable and laid my eyes on Jaundis and Tally for the first time in a year. They looked just as beautiful as the day I'd left them. I rolled over and opened their compartment doors. With the newly built fence I would no longer need to keep them in the stalls all day and night as I had been doing. I watched them as they slowly walked out most curiously.

THE END

www.ingramcontent.com/pod-product-compliance
Lightning Source LLC
Chambersburg PA
CBHW070236290526
45789CB00004B/1650